Read & Respond

Ages 7–11

SECTION 1
This Morning I Met a Whale
Teachers' notes ....

SECTION 2
Guided reading
Teachers' notes 4

SECTION 3
Shared reading
Teachers' notes 7
Photocopiable extracts 8

SECTION 4
Plot, character and setting
Activity notes 11
Photocopiable activities 15

SECTION 5
Talk about it
Activity notes 19
Photocopiable activities 22

SECTION 6
Get writing
Activity notes 25
Photocopiable activities 28

SECTION 7
Assessment
Teachers' notes and activity 31
Photocopiable activity 32

READ & RESPOND: Activities based on This Morning I Met a Whale

Read & Respond

Ages 7–11

Author: Jillian Powell

Commissioning Editor: Rachel Mackinnon

Development Editor: Marion Archer

Editor: Margaret Eaton

Assistant Editor: Rachel Coombs

Series Designer: Anna Oliwa

Designer: Anna Oliwa

Illustrations: Mike Phillips (Beehive Illustration)

Text © 2012, Jillian Powell © 2012, Scholastic Ltd

Designed using Adobe InDesign

Published by Scholastic Ltd,
Book End, Range Road, Witney,
Oxfordshire OX29 0YD
www.scholastic.co.uk

Printed by Bell & Bain
1 2 3 4 5 6 7 8 9   2 3 4 5 6 7 8 9 0 1

British Library Cataloguing-in-Publication Data
A catalogue record for this book is available from
the British Library.

ISBN 978-1407-12730-9

The rights of Jillian Powell to be identified as the author of this work have been asserted by her in accordance with the Copyright, Designs and Patents Act 1988.

Extracts from the Primary National Strategy's Primary Framework for Literacy (2006)   nationalstrategies.standards.dcsf.gov.uk/primary/primaryframework/literacyframework © Crown copyright. Reproduced under the terms of the Click Use Licence.

All rights reserved. This book is sold subject to the condition that it shall not, by way of trade or otherwise, be lent, hired out or otherwise circulated without the publisher's prior consent in any form of binding or cover other than that in which it is published and without a similar condition, including this condition, being imposed upon the subsequent purchaser.

No part of this publication may be reproduced, stored in a retrieval system, or transmitted, in any form or by any means, electronic, mechanical, photocopying, recording or otherwise, without the prior permission of the publisher. This book remains copyright, although permission is granted to copy pages where indicated for classroom distribution and use only in the school which has purchased the book, or by the teacher who has purchased the book, and in accordance with the CLA licensing agreement. Photocopying permission is given only for purchasers and not for borrowers of books from any lending service.

Acknowledgements

The publishers gratefully acknowledge permission to reproduce the following copyright material: **David Higham Associates** for the use of text extracts from *This Morning I Met a Whale* by Michael Morpurgo. Text © 2008, Michael Morpurgo (2008, Walker Books). **Walker Book**s for the use of the cover from *This Morning I Met a Whale* by Michael Morpurgo, illustrated by Christian Birmingham. Cover illustration © 2008, Christian Birmingham (2008, Walker Books). Every effort has been made to trace copyright holders for the works reproduced in this book, and the publishers apologise for any inadvertent omissions.

This Morning I Met a Whale

SECTION 1

About the book

Michael Morpurgo has said his novels are inspired by real-life events – little happenings, big happenings, history. *This Morning I Met a Whale* was inspired by a 'big happening' in London in the winter of 2006, when a five-metre bottle-nosed whale swam up the River Thames as far as Battersea Bridge, where she became stranded. Rescuers battled to save her for two days, but she died before the rescue pontoon on which they were carrying her could reach the open sea.

The novel narrates the events through the eyes of Michael, a young boy whose hobby of bird-watching takes him down to the shores of the River Thames at sunrise, allowing him to be the first person to see the whale. This whale has come with a purpose: to find an open-minded child who will listen and pass on its warning that humans are recklessly killing their world. Nature and environmental issues are frequent themes in Morpurgo's novels: the rescue of wild animals features in *Why the Whales Came*, *The Wreck of the Zanzibar* and *Kensuke's Kingdom*.

In this novel, the animals are given their own voice through the whale which addresses Michael, warning him that humans must put right the damage they are doing to the planet, its climate, seas and endangered species. Michael must promise to pass its message on to the world, but when he reads his story in class at school, no one – not even his teacher – believes him. All are astonished when news reaches the media that there really is a whale in the Thames. Michael then becomes involved in the desperate efforts to rescue the whale, swimming alongside it towards the open sea, until it becomes clear that the whale is dying, and all he can do is fulfil his promise to relay its vital message to the world.

About the author

Born in St Albans in 1943, Michael Morpurgo grew up in aftermath of the Second World War. He was not an academic child at school, but always enjoyed reading, especially the works of Robert Louis Stevenson, Rudyard Kipling and later, the poet Ted Hughes. He was in the army for a short period before becoming a teacher, which inspired him to write as he realised he found 'a kind of magic' in telling stories to the children in his class.

Morpurgo has always had a passionate concern for nature and the environment. He believes that instilling a sense of awareness of the environment in children will encourage them to take responsibility for its care – an idea that is also fundamental to the charity *Farms for City Children* that he founded with his wife in 1976.

Michael Morpurgo has written over 120 books. He has had many novels adapted for stage and film (including the hugely successful stage play and film, *War Horse*). He was awarded the OBE in 2006, and was Children's Laureate from 2003 to 2005.

Facts and figures
First published in 2008 by Walker Books.
Michael Morpurgo has won many awards including The Smarties Book Prize (*The Butterfly Lion*), The Whitbread Prize (*The Wreck of the Zanzibar*) and the Children's Book of the Year Award (*Kensuke's Kingdom* and *Private Peaceful*).

Guided reading

SECTION 2

First reading

The first reading of the book should be used to familiarise the children with the story and introduce the key themes and ideas.

Expectations

Look together at the cover of the book. Ask the children what they think the story is about – what do they learn from the title and illustration? (The *I* is a boy, watching a whale swimming upriver.) Now turn to the back cover and read the blurb together. Ask the children what more they have learned about the story. Turn to the author's note (final page of the book), and read it together. Ask the children if any of them can recall hearing or seeing news stories about stranded whales.

First section

Begin reading the story, pausing to look at the first double-page illustration. Identify Battersea Bridge over the Thames in London, and the time of day: dawn, which creates a quiet, magical mood. Read on to *I was doing the same*, then turn the page and ask: *Why was the river holding its breath?* (A whale is coming.) Identify the bottle nose and fins. Continue reading as far as *I was just about ready to run off*. Pause to look at the next illustration and ask what we have learned about the whale. (He has come on a mission to find Michael, having made a promise to his grandfather.) Identify the only figures in the scene (Michael, the whale and the egret).

Continue reading as far as *bridges and towers and spires*. Can the children identify the city and, if so, how? (It is London, because of the red buses.) Read on, identifying Tower Bridge in the illustration on the next page. Continue reading to *...tell us his story*, then ask the children to explain why the whale has been looking for a child. (This is because children rescued his grandfather and he knows they have open minds and will listen.)

Now read to the end of the boy's story, where it says *And that's the end of my story*. Pause to examine the remaining illustrations in this section, notice the shift in page colour and mood as Michael 'travels' in his head with the whale. Ask the children: *What is the whale's warning?* (That humans are destroying the planet.) *What does Michael have to promise?* (To pass on the message in a race against time to save the world.)

Second section

Begin reading from *Mrs Fergusson was so delighted...* Invite the children to identify the shift in narrative: from first person to third person. Read as far as *"An amazing story, Michael..."*. Ask the children why they think Michael has written his story. (He made a promise to the whale to pass on his message.) Point out that the first part of the novel is Michael's story, written in his own words.

Continue to *"I'm not a liar,"* and look at the following illustration. Ask: *What problem does Michael face?* (No one believes him; they think he is making it all up.) *Would you believe him? What makes it hard to believe?* (That a whale would be in the middle of London, and that it talks to him.)

Read on to *Do it for them. Do it for me*. Ask the children to explain why the whale is now in danger. (The tide has receded so it is almost beached in the shallows.) Read as far as *He ran all the way back down to the river* and pause to look at the following illustration, this time evocative of the quiet and magic of night. Read on to the end of *the barge was the whale's only chance of survival*. Ask the children: *Do you find this passage realistic, or does the story enter the realms of adventure/ fantasy here, with a small boy swimming alongside the whale at night?*

Complete the story, reminding the children that some of these events really did happen in January 2006, when rescuers failed to save a bottle-nosed whale that had swum up the River Thames. What does Michael understand that the vet does not? (Why the whale came, and what his mission was.) Allow the children time to reflect on the ending. How does it make them feel? Do they think a sad ending is effective and, if so, why? (The whale has carried out his mission

Guided reading

SECTION 2

but has paid with his life, leaving us all to heed his warning and make sure we put things right.)

Second reading

Use subsequent readings to allow the children to explore the text and illustrations in more depth. As they already know the storyline, they can now concentrate on different aspects, such as themes, text features and illustrations.

Narrative structure

Allow time to establish an overview of the way the novel is structured. Point out that there are no chapter numbers, but that the author indicates shifts in time or narrative using other devices – for example, a shift from first to third person narrative, change in background page colour and italicised text.

Consider how Michael's first-person narrative is effectively 'a story within a story' and can be seen as the story he writes out in class, which his teacher reads to the children. Invite the children to speculate why the author shifts the narrative from the first person to the third person. Why has he used first-person 'diary' or 'memoir' form to describe Michael's encounter? (Perhaps to give it immediacy and impact and, because we are being asked to suspend disbelief about a talking whale, it is more convincing that Michael tells us himself.) What does shifting to a third-person narrative in the second part of the story add or enable? (The narrator can provide a wider perspective of the scene and events, describing details such as the builder on his mobile phone, the egret that follows the whale out to sea, and so on.)

Identify the central section of the story from *He showed me...* to *She wasn't crying, because she was dead*, which takes Michael on a global journey through the whale's eyes, describing some of the key environmental issues that are threatening the planet. Discuss how the author uses a few key scenes to represent issues. (The orang-utans show endangered wildlife and the polar bear on the melting ice cap represents climate change.)

Illustrations

Consider the role of Christian Birmingham's illustrations, which are a significant and integral part of this novel. Encourage the children to explore and describe them, examining the soft, impressionistic effect of the pastels, and the way the artist uses light and dark to create mood (first double-page illustration) or drama (ninth double-page illustration).

Invite the children to explore the purpose and effect of the 'stand alone' double-page illustrations and how they function. For example, they reflect and contribute to the mood of the narrative (as on the first double-page illustration where Michael is describing the magical quality of dawn by the river). They also anticipate or foreshadow events in the text, as in the second double-page illustration where the whale appears in the illustration before the narrative describes it. In addition, they help to describe setting and events (as on the twelfth and thirteenth double-page illustrations).

Treatment

Consider how the author has interpreted and adapted the real-life events: a bottle-nosed whale really did swim up the Thames and died after desperate attempts to rescue it failed. In the novel, he answers the question 'What was a whale doing swimming up the Thames?' by investing it with a purpose or mission (to pass on its warning about the damage humans are inflicting on their planet). The whale is literally given a voice in that it speaks to Michael to pass on its message. Discuss the 'licence' with which the real-life events are treated: would a young boy really have been allowed by the police and other authorities to wade in the river at night-time and swim alongside the whale? What does this add to the narrative? (Heroism, adventure, a sense of the strong bond between boy and whale.)

Consider the character of Michael and why the whale has chosen him. (He is young, open-minded, interested in nature and the environment.) Encourage the children to think how Michael is in some ways an ordinary boy (he

Guided reading

SECTION 2

eats pizza and watches television, he feels upset when his classmates laugh at him), but he also becomes a heroic character, wading out to swim alongside the whale. He alone is charged with passing on the whale's message to humans, in a race to save a dying planet.

Reflect together on the ending, and why the author chooses to have a sad ending, relating how the whale dies as it did in real life, rather than changing the story so that the whale survives. How would a happy ending have altered the impact? Does it make the whale's message more poignant, in that it sacrificed itself to carry its message to a child? Point out that it also leaves Michael (significantly, the author's namesake) solely responsible for passing on the message.

Invite the children to recall any other books by the author that have carried environmental themes or messages (for example, *Kensuke's Kingdom, Why the Whales Came, The Wreck of the Zanzibar*). Explain to the class that the author believes it is important to raise awareness of environmental issues in children so that they will become responsible guardians for our planet.

Shared reading

SECTION 3

Extract 1

- Read an enlarged copy of the first extract. Discuss how effective this is as an opening to a novel. Underline the first sentence and discuss its impact. Suggest that it sounds improbable and fantastical but that the narrator then provides detail of time and place.
- Ask the children to pick out all the words or phrases that establish time of day (*five o'clock, first light, dawn chorus, sunrise*) and place (*river, Battersea*).
- Discuss why the time and place are important to the storyline: Michael is the first person to see the whale swimming up the River Thames. What effect would be lost if it was midday, with the river busy? (Others might see the whale, it might not get the chance to talk to him and pass on its message.)
- Ask the children: *What do we learn about Michael in this opening passage?* (He is a keen bird-watcher and loves observing nature.)
- Focus on the description of the heron. Challenge the children to find two similes (*like lightning, like pteradactyls*) and to explain what they suggest.

Extract 2

- Read an enlarged copy of Extract 2. Ask: *Who is speaking?* (The whale.) What is he describing? (His grandfather's journey up the River Thames.)
- Underline the words *narwhals* and *beached* and ask the children if they can explain them. (A type of whale, and getting stranded in shallow water.)
- Highlight the word *warning* and ask the children to explain how this would have occurred. (Through whale song, or whales communicating to each other.)
- Ask the children to identify the city and explain the clue. (London, because of its red buses.) Discuss how this is a 'whale's eye' view of the city, as seen from the river; ask the children to pick out all the river features (*cranes, docks, wharfs, boats, barges, bridges*). Focus on river barges, and challenge the children to think of some river words (for example, 'river banks', 'current', 'bed', 'channel', 'delta', 'boat').
- Can the children explain why the river is dangerous as well as wonderful to Grandfather? (As he ventures further upstream, he could become stranded in shallow water, or collide with boats or barges.)

Extract 3

- Read an enlarged copy of Extract 3. Encourage the children to describe what is happening. (Michael is swimming alongside the whale in the River Thames, to try to encourage it to reach the safety of the open sea.)
- Ask: *What makes it so difficult for boy and whale?* (The tide is against them and they are both exhausted.) Challenge the children to define what the *tide* means. (The rise and fall of water in oceans, seas and rivers due to the effect of the Moon and Sun on the Earth.)
- Invite the children to pick out all the words that emphasise how hard the struggle is, and circle them (such as, *hard, puffing and blowing, battling, impossible, tired, struggle*). Can they identify what part of speech each word is? (Adjective, participle verbs, adjective, verb, noun.)
- Challenge the class to think of some more words for each part of speech that suggest struggle (for example, adjective: 'tiring', 'strenuous', 'arduous'; verb: 'fighting', 'endeavouring'; noun: 'battle', 'fight' and 'effort').

Shared reading

Extract 1

This morning I met a whale. It was just after five o'clock and I was down by the river. Sometimes, when my alarm clock works, and when I feel like it, I get up early, because I like to go bird-watching, because bird-watching is my favourite hobby. I usually go just before first light. Mum doesn't mind, just so long as I don't wake her up, just so long as I'm back for breakfast.

It's the best time. You get to hear the dawn chorus. You get to see the sunrise and the whole world waking up around you. That's when the birds come flying down to the river to feed, and I can watch them landing in the water. I love that. If you're already there when they come, they hardly notice you, and then you don't bother them. Hardly anyone else is down by the river at five o'clock, sometimes no one at all, just the birds and me. The rest of London is asleep. Well, mostly anyway.

From our flat in Battersea it takes about five minutes to walk down to the river. The first bird I saw this morning was a heron. I love herons because they stand so still in the shallows. They're looking for fish, waiting to strike. When they strike they do it so fast, it's like lightning, and when they catch something they look so surprised and so pleased with themselves, as if they've never done it before. When they walk they walk in slow motion. When they take off and fly they look prehistoric, like pterodactyls almost. Herons are my best.

Shared reading

SECTION 3

Extract 2

"...Grandfather had gone off to explore an unknown river, to follow it inland as far as he could go. No other whale had ever before dared to go there, as far as anyone knew anyway. All he knew of this river was that a couple of narwhals had been beached there in the mouth of the river a long time ago. They never made it back out to sea. The warning had gone out all over the oceans, and that was why whales had avoided the river ever since.

"It took a while for Grandfather to find it, but when he did he just kept on swimming. On and on he swam right into the middle of the biggest city he'd ever seen. It was teeming with life. Everywhere he looked there were great cranes leaning out over the river, and towering wharfs and busy docks. Everywhere there were boats and barges. He saw cars and trains and great red buses. And at night the lights were so bright that the whole sky was bright with them. It was a magical city, a place of bridges and towers and spires. And everywhere there were people, crowds of them, more than he'd ever seen before, more than he'd ever imagined there could be. He wanted to stay longer, to explore further upstream, to discover more. It was a wonderful place, but Grandfather knew it was dangerous too.

Shared reading

Extract 3

From the bank they all saw it, Michael and the whale swimming away side by side towards Battersea Bridge. They could hardly believe their eyes. They could see the whale was finding it hard, puffing and blowing as he went, that Michael was battling against the tide. But incredibly, they were both making some headway. By now the rescue team had sent out an inflatable to fetch Michael in. Everyone could see what was bound to happen in the end, that the tide was against them, that it was too cold, that it was impossible. Both the boy and the whale tired together. They hauled Michael out of the water, and brought him back to the shore. From there he had to watch his whale swim on bravely for a few more minutes, before he had to give up the unequal struggle. Even Michael knew now that there was nothing more he could do, that the barge was the whale's only chance of survival.

Plot, character and setting

SECTION 4

Global journey

Objective: To identify and summarise evidence from a text to support a hypothesis.
What you need: Copies of *This Morning I Met a Whale*, whiteboard, individual whiteboards and pens.

What to do

- Re-read from *He showed me...* to *...She wasn't crying, because she was dead*. With the class, note how the text is differentiated by the background page colour and discuss why. (To separate out the text in which the whale takes Michael on a global journey in his mind.)
- Ask: *What is it that the whale wants Michael to see and understand?* (How humans are damaging the environment and wildlife that shares their planet.)
- Arrange the children into pairs. Invite them to scan through the text and complete two columns on their whiteboards, one with the heading 'Location' and the other 'Environmental issue'. The children should list all the locations and species or issues that the whale shows Michael. For example: Location – The Arctic; Environmental issue – Climate change (melting of the polar ice caps).
- Allow the children time to scan the text and note down all the different locations and issues that the whale refers to.
- When they have finished, encourage pairs to discuss any other issues that the whale could have described, and add them to the columns. For example: Seas – over-fishing/exhaustion of fish stocks; pollution from industrial waste, nuclear accidents; Africa – poaching elephants for ivory; Asia – hunting whales for meat and oil.

Differentiation
For older/more confident learners: Encourage the children to research more environmental issues to add to their lists.
For younger/less confident learners: Provide a list of prompt words to help the children add issues (for example, drought, floods, poaching, over-fishing, pollution, hunger/starvation).

Landmarks

Objective: To identify and summarise evidence from a text to support a hypothesis.
What you need: Copies of *This Morning I Met a Whale*, whiteboard and photocopiable page 15.
Cross-curricular link: Geography.

What to do

- Ask the children: *Where is the story set?* (London, by the River Thames at Battersea.)
- Challenge the children to name some London landmarks that feature in the story, either in the text or illustrations, and write them on the whiteboard (Battersea Bridge, Tower Bridge, the River Thames, and so on).
- Arrange the children into small groups. Tell them to scan the story and write down all the London sights they can find.
- When they have compiled their lists, hand out photocopiable page 15 and ask the groups to work together to complete it.
- Once they have done this, bring the class back together and share ideas. Challenge the children to add more ideas to each section from their own knowledge. (For example, bicycles for transport, or the Millennium Bridge for bridges.)

Differentiation
For older/more confident learners: Encourage groups to do their own research on London, adding their ideas to the photocopiable sheet.
For younger/less confident children: Let the children concentrate on just two sections on the photocopiable sheet (for example, transport and bridges).

READ & RESPOND: Activities based on *This Morning I Met a Whale*

Plot, character and setting

SECTION 4

Truth or fiction?

> **Objective:** To interrogate texts to deepen and clarify understanding and response.
> **What you need:** Copies of *This Morning I Met a Whale*, whiteboard, individual whiteboards and pens.
> **Cross-curricular link:** History.

What to do
- Re-read together the author's note at the back of the book. Ask the children to suggest one detail about the whale in the story that is based on the real historical event, and one that is fiction. For example: 'A whale swam up the River Thames' (true); 'The whale talked to a boy called Michael' (fiction).
- Arrange the children into pairs. One child should note down all the details about the whale in the story that are based on real historical events, such as: 'A bottle-nosed whale swam up the River Thames. It reached Battersea Bridge. A rescue attempt was made. It died before they could reach the sea.' The other child should list all the details in the story that are fictional: 'The whale was male. It had come on a mission to pass on a message. It was re-tracing its grandfather's journey. It talked to Michael.'
- When the pairs have finished, bring the class together to reflect how the author has changed certain details to create an exciting storyline.

> **Differentiation**
> **For older/more confident learners:** Encourage pairs of children to research more details about the events in 2006 and decide whether the author has used or changed them.
> **For younger/less confident learners:** Let pairs work together to compile just one of the lists.

An ordinary boy?

> **Objective:** To infer characters' feelings in fiction.
> **What you need:** Copies of *This Morning I Met a Whale*, individual whiteboards, pens and photocopiable page 16.
> **Cross-curricular link:** PSHE.

What to do
- Ask the children to focus on the character of Michael, and think of all the things that make him an ordinary boy, and all the things that make him special.
- Arrange the children into pairs and tell them to use their whiteboards to compile their lists under two headings. For example:
  - Michael is an ordinary boy: (He goes to school every day; He doesn't like writing in class; He gets into fights with a class mate.)
  - Michael is special: (The whale seeks him out; He hears a whale talk; He swims alone alongside the whale.)
- When they have finished this task, provide each pair with a copy of photocopiable page 16. Ask them to write down what each character might say about Michael. Encourage them to think about motivation and interaction with Michael. For example, the vet might be surprised and impressed by Michael's bond with the whale.

> **Differentiation**
> **For older/more confident learners:** Encourage the children to add another speech bubble on the reverse side of the photocopiable sheet, and use it to write something Michael might say about himself.
> **For younger/less confident learners:** Let these children concentrate on two or three speech bubbles only.

Plot, character and setting

SECTION 4

In pictures

Objective: To identify features that writers use to provoke readers' reactions.
What you need: Copies of *This Morning I Met a Whale*, individual whiteboards and pens.
Cross-curricular link: Art and design.

What to do
- Tell the children they are going to focus on the illustrations and how they contribute to the story.
- Arrange the children into pairs. Ask them to scan through the book and choose one illustration to explore further. They should discuss together:
  - What can we see in the picture?
  - How does it reflect or add to the narrative?
  - How would we describe the mood?
- The children should then decide how they could annotate their picture with key names, events or ideas. (For example, Battersea Bridge, the River Thames, Michael talking to the whale, the egret.)
- Let them sketch out their ideas for annotation using labels, then ask for volunteers to present their picture to the class, explaining how they

Differentiation
For older/more confident learners: Encourage the children to add explanations to labelled detail – for example, the whale reaches as far as Battersea Bridge, or the egret watches over the whale and Michael, and stays with the rescue attempt.
For younger/less confident learners: Allow the children to concentrate on describing what the illustration shows and how it reflects or adds to the narrative.

In the news

Objective: To interrogate texts to deepen and clarify understanding and response.
What you need: Copies of *This Morning I Met a Whale*, whiteboard, individual whiteboards, pens and photocopiable page 17.
Cross-curricular links: Citizenship, history.

What to do
- Referring to the author's note at the back of the book, remind the children that the novel is based on a true news story.
- Tell them that an effective news report should answer the five 'W's – who, what, where, when, why.
- Write these five headings on the whiteboard. Arrange the children into pairs and tell them to copy the headings onto their individual whiteboards and then try to fill in answers about the novel. For example:
  - Who: a bottle-nosed whale and a boy called Michael.
  - What: the whale swam up the River Thames and became stranded.
  - Where: near Battersea Bridge in London.
  - When: at sunrise, one morning in winter.
  - Why: to ask Michael to pass on a warning to humans.
- Allow the children time to fill in all the answers on their whiteboards.
- Provide each pair with photocopiable page 17. Tell them to plan a newspaper story about the rescue attempt that answers all five 'W's using words and pictures. They can use the notes on their whiteboards as a checklist.

Differentiation
For older/more confident learners: Invite the children to develop their news stories using ICT skills.
For younger/less confident learners: Review the five 'W's as a shared activity and allow the children to concentrate on three of the five 'W's.

Plot, character and setting

SECTION 4

Timeline

Objective: To identify and make notes of the main points of section(s) of text.
What you need: Copies of *This Morning I Met a Whale*, whiteboard, individual whiteboards and pens.
Cross-curricular link: History.

What to do
- Ask the children to consider how much time they think the story spans. Encourage them to cite evidence using both the text and illustrations, asking: *What time of day is it when the story begins?* (Sunrise.) *What time of day is it when it ends?* (Night-time.)
- Arrange the children into pairs. Tell them they are going to plot a timeline for the day, from sunrise to night-time, marking in when they think key events occur.
- Suggest that they scan through the text first, listing events: Michael spots the whale, the whale talks to him, Michael goes to school and writes his essay, the headmaster reports the whale in the river, and so on. They should then plot these events on the timeline.
- When they have finished, bring the class back together and discuss which episodes are fast moving (for example, when the children rush down to the river to see the whale) and which are slower moving (such as when the whale is talking to Michael). Invite the children to consider how the author varies the pace, with some slower, more reflective passages and some with fast-moving action.

Differentiation
For older/more confident learners: Encourage the children to include as much detail as they can – such as Michael eating pizza and watching television in the evening.
For younger/less confident learners: Compile a list of key events on the whiteboard as a shared activity, then ask pairs to plot them on a timeline.

Amazing whale

Objective: To deduce characters' reasons for behaviour from their actions.
What you need: Copies of *This Morning I Met a Whale*, whiteboard and photocopiable page 18.
Cross-curricular link: Science.

What to do
- Challenge the children to brainstorm words or phrases to describe the whale (such as 'huge', 'strong', 'brave', 'courageous', 'caring', 'clever'). Encourage them to think about his behaviour as well as his appearance. List their ideas on the whiteboard.
- Ask volunteers to explain why they chose their word. For example:
  - The whale is brave because he might get stranded and die.
  - The whale is clever because he has found his way to London.
- Discuss which words or phrases on the list might apply to whales generally (such as 'huge', 'strong', 'clever') and which to this whale in particular (perhaps 'caring' and 'brave').
- Finally, hand out photocopiable page 18 and ask the children to complete the sheet using their knowledge of the whale in the novel.

Differentiation
For older/more confident learners: Challenge the children to write further statements about the whale to add to the photocopiable sheet, citing evidence from the book to support their statements.
For younger/less confident learners: Let the children work in pairs to complete three of the statements on the photocopiable sheet.

Plot, character and setting

Landmarks

- In the table below write details about London as described in the text and illustrations of the book.

The river	
Bridges	
Transport	
Industry	
River wildlife	

Plot, character and setting

SECTION 4

An ordinary boy?

- Write what each of these characters might say about Michael.

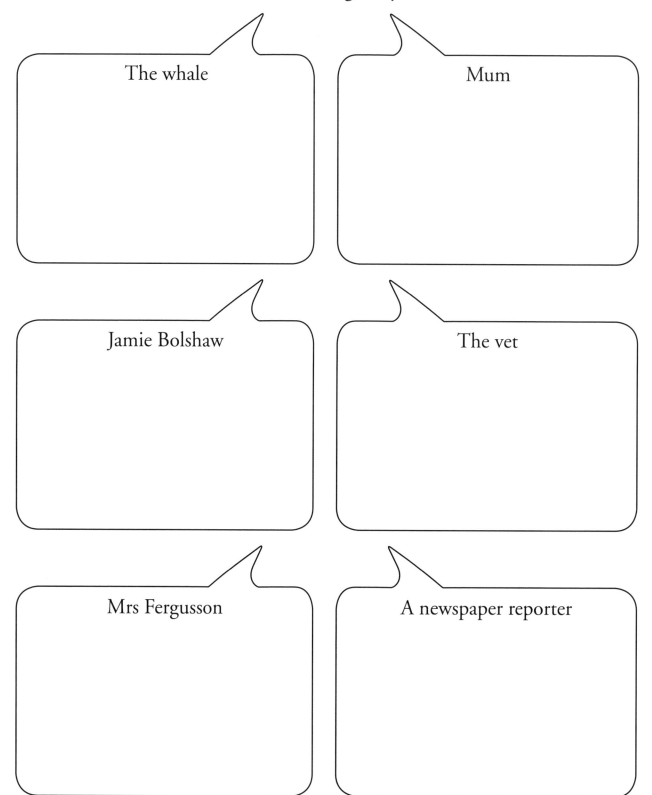

Plot, character and setting

SECTION 4

In the news

- Plan a newspaper story that reports the whale rescue attempt. Make sure your report answers all the five 'W's (who, what, where, when and why).

YOUR DAILY News   20p

Report headline:

_____

Summarise the content of your report:

_____
_____
_____
_____
_____

Brief for a photograph to accompany your report:

What might two eyewitnesses say when interviewed?

The vet

Building worker in crowd

Plot, character and setting

SECTION 4

Amazing whale

● Write down evidence from the novel that tells us the following information about the whale.

1. The whale is friendly towards Michael.
   _____
   _____

2. The whale knows the risks it is taking.
   _____
   _____

3. The whale knows he has an important mission to carry out.
   _____
   _____

4. The whale keeps his promises.
   _____
   _____

5. The whale needs Michael's help.
   _____
   _____

6. The whale is too weak to return to the sea.
   _____
   _____

Talk about it

SECTION 5

A favourite hobby

Objective: To present information, ensuring that items are clearly sequenced, relevant details are included and accounts are ended effectively.
What you need: Copies of *This Morning I Met a Whale* and photocopiable page 22.
Cross-curricular link: PSHE.

What to do
- Remind the children that Michael encounters the whale because he is down by the river at sunrise, pursuing his favourite hobby.
- Re-read at pace from the beginning of the story as far as *I couldn't take my eyes off him.*
- Ask the children: *What does Michael love to do?* (Go birdwatching by the River Thames.) *Why does he get up so early?* (That is when the birds come to feed, and he can hear the dawn chorus.) *What skills or attributes do you think a birdwatcher needs?* (They need to be quiet, patient and observant.)
- Hand out photocopiable page 22 and explain to the children that they are going to describe their own favourite pastime or hobby, and explain why they like it.
- Allow the children time to complete the photocopiable sheet, then invite volunteers to talk briefly about their favourite hobby, using their notes. Encourage questions and answers about each hobby.

Differentiation
For older/more confident learners: Encourage the children to make presentations to the class about their hobby, without referring to notes.
For younger/less confident learners: Let the children concentrate on providing one reason why they enjoy their hobby and limit questioning from the class.

Big issues

Objective: To offer reasons and evidence for their views, considering alternative opinions.
What you need: Copies of *This Morning I Met a Whale*, whiteboard, individual whiteboards and pens.
Cross-curricular links: Science, geography.

What to do
- Focus on the whale's description of the issues that the planet is facing, re-reading from *He showed me the bottom of the sea…* as far as *Will you do that?*
- Challenge the children to identify the big issues underlying each scene that the whale shows Michael and list them on the whiteboard. For example:
  - Pollution of the seas is killing the coral reef.
  - Fishing boats are using huge nets that trap and kill sea creatures.
  - Climate change is melting the ice cap and endangering polar bears.
- Arrange the class into groups. Assign each group one of the identified issues (pollution, climate change, destruction of wildlife habitats, hunting and poaching of endangered species, war and killing). Challenge each group to discuss their issue, and come up with three constructive ideas for how humans could change their ways or make things better.
- Once the groups have completed their discussions, bring the class together to share ideas. Make a note of the best ideas on the whiteboard.

Differentiation
For older/more confident learners: Encourage the children to review shared ideas and expand the list of ideas for one or more issues.
For younger/less confident learners: Allow the children to concentrate on one big issue and focus on what we can each do to try to change things for the better.

Talk about it

SECTION 5

Michael's promise

Objective: To follow up others' points and show whether they agree or disagree in whole-class discussion.
What you need: Copies of *This Morning I Met a Whale* and whiteboard.
Cross-curricular link: Science.

What to do
- Read with the class from *Grandfather said all this killing...* to *Will you do that?* Focus on the whale's instructions. Ask the children: *What has the whale asked Michael to do?* (Pass on his warning about the damage that humans are doing to the planet.)
- Arrange the class into small groups. Invite the children to imagine they are Michael and to discuss the following questions: How would they go about this mission if they were Michael? Who could he tell? What would he say? How would he get his message across? How could he show people they have to change the way they live?
- Suggest that the novel is one way of passing on the whale's message: can the children think of other methods?
- Allow the groups sufficient time for discussion, then bring the class together and encourage volunteers from each group to share ideas.
- Note the best ideas on the whiteboard, encouraging feedback and criticism. Then compile a class strategy for how Michael could act on his promise.

Differentiation
For older/more confident learners: Encourage the children to consider how Michael could use social media and technology to reach a wider audience.
For younger/less confident learners: Let the children concentrate on discussing how the novel is one way of passing on the whale's message, and to consider one other method that Michael could use.

Talking animals

Objective: To use some drama strategies to explore stories or issues.
What you need: Copies of *This Morning I Met a Whale* and photocopiable page 23.
Cross-curricular link: Drama.

What to do
- Begin by re-reading from *An amazing story...* to *"Yeah, yeah," Jamie sneered*. Ask the class: *How would you react to a classmate reading a story like this? Do you think you would believe them?*
- Provide each child with photocopiable page 23 and ask them to invent a similar scenario in which an animal talks to them and tells them a secret or gives them a message. They can use their imagination to decide what sort of animal it is, what it says and where the event takes place. Encourage the children to include any detail that might convince others, and discuss what this might be. (For example, detail about the animal's appearance or voice, or something that happens while it is talking to them, such as when the whale sprays Michael with water when its tail thrashes.)
- Allow time for the children to fill in the photocopiable sheet, then invite volunteers to present their ideas orally to the class.
- Encourage feedback from the class. Which are the most convincing ideas and why? What makes the description persuasive – what helps us believe the speaker? (Vivid or unusual detail? Persuasive language?)

Differentiation
For older/more confident learners: Encourage the children to suggest how they would develop their scenario into a storyline.
For younger/less confident learners: Let the children work in pairs to invent a scenario and allow them to concentrate on describing the animal's appearance and the message it passes on.

Talk about it

News report

Objective: To use some drama strategies to explore stories or issues.
What you need: Copies of *This Morning I Met a Whale*, individual whiteboards and pens.
Cross-curricular link: Drama.

What to do
- Explain to the children they are going to prepare and present a television news report about the whale and the rescue attempt.
- Arrange the class into small groups. Invite each group to choose members to play a TV presenter, the vet, Michael, a diver and an onlooker.
- The children should scan the novel from *It's on the telly...* to the end of the story, noting key details on their whiteboards, such as the crowds, police, divers and barge. Ask them to pinpoint the time and location of their report (for example, when the whale is being lifted onto the barge), then improvise what the presenter and interviewees will say.
- Allow each group time to rehearse their report, then invite one or two groups to perform in front of the class.
- Encourage constructive feedback from the children. How informative was the report? How could it have been edited or improved?

Differentiation
For older/more confident learners: Encourage the children to use their ICT skills to record and broadcast their report.
For younger/less confident learners: Provide the children with page references to help pinpoint key details, the time and location before they begin improvising.

Illustration brief

Objective: To select and use a range of technical and descriptive vocabulary.
What you need: Copies of *This Morning I Met a Whale*, whiteboard and photocopiable page 24.
Cross-curricular link: Art and design.

What to do
- Inform the children that, in this lesson, they are going to focus on the illustrations and write a brief for another double-page illustration that could feature in the book.
- Arrange the children into pairs and provide them with photocopiable page 24. Explain that they should first scan through the text and choose an event or moment that could be illustrated across two pages.
- With the class, discuss a few ideas and write them on the whiteboard, such as a scene showing the children rescuing the whale's grandfather, or Michael's whale being lifted onto the barge. Encourage the children to consider the style and content of the other illustrations in the book, and how their picture will fit into the story overall.
- Allow the pairs sufficient time to complete the sheet, then bring the class together and invite volunteers to describe where their illustration will appear in the novel and what it will show.

Differentiation
For older/more confident learners: Challenge the children to create two illustration briefs and to describe the proposed content and style of illustration without referring to their notes.
For younger/less confident learners: Allow the children to concentrate on presenting a sketch of their illustration to the class, pointing out its key content and style features.

Talk about it

SECTION 5

A favourite hobby

- Describe your favourite pastime or hobby.

The hobby I like best is:
_____
_____

I usually do my hobby (Where? When?):
_____
_____

The skills I need for my hobby are:
_____
_____

The equipment or materials I need for my hobby are:
_____
_____

Three reasons why I enjoy my hobby:

1. _____
_____

2. _____
_____

3. _____
_____

PHOTOCOPIABLE

Talk about it

SECTION 5

Talking animals

● Imagine you meet an animal that talks to you when you are alone and tells you a secret or message.

Describe the animal you encounter.

_____
_____
_____

What does the animal say?

_____
_____
_____

How does the animal's voice sound?

_____
_____
_____

What does the animal ask you to do?

_____
_____
_____

Who do you tell and what do you say to convince them you are telling the truth?

_____
_____
_____

Talk about it

Illustration brief

- Write a detailed brief for a new double-page illustration to include in *This Morning I Met a Whale*.

Summarise the text your picture will illustrate.

_____
_____
_____
_____
_____

Sketch your picture here.

Briefly outline the content of your picture.
(Panorama? Close-up? Scenery? Action? Figures?)

_____
_____
_____
_____
_____
_____

What mood will your picture capture?

_____
_____
_____
_____

Get writing

SECTION 6

Bird-spotter's guide

Objective: To select and use a range of technical and descriptive vocabulary.
What you need: Copies of *This Morning I Met a Whale* and photocopiable page 28.
Cross-curricular links: Science, geography.

What to do
- Challenge the children to cite birds that Michael has seen by the river, and list them on the whiteboard. (Heron, egret, moorhen, coot, crested grebe, swan, cormorant and duck.) Which is his favourite and why? (Herons because he loves watching them fish and take off in flight.)
- Explain to the children that they are going to write entries for a bird-spotter's guide that Michael might use. Before they begin, discuss the type of information that such a guide might include – facts on size and appearance, habitat, diet, behaviour, and so on.
- Arrange the class into small groups and hand out photocopiable page 28. Assign each group one type of waterbird to research and allow them time to find out information about it using books or the internet. They should use the information to complete the photocopiable sheet.
- When they have finished, allow the children to work individually to draft a paragraph about their bird. Invite volunteers to read their paragraphs to the class. Encourage constructive feedback: which paragraphs are most informative or well-constructed and why?

Differentiation
For older/more confident learners: Encourage the children to develop their entry for a bird-spotter's guide using ICT skills and challenge them to write two or more paragraphs.
For younger/less confident learners: Limit the children to focus on appearance, habitat and diet. Then allow them to work in pairs to draft a short paragraph about the bird.

Whale on a mission

Objective: To use settings and characterisation to engage readers' interest.
What you need: Copies of *This Morning I Met a Whale*, whiteboard, individual whiteboards and pens.

What to do
- Read together from *Then I spotted something…* to *I stood there for ages and ages*. Ask the children: *Why does the whale choose Michael?* (He is looking for an open-minded child. Michael is interested in nature and birdwatching.)
- Tell the children they are going to rewrite this part of the story from the whale's point of view. Encourage them to consider how the whale is feeling. Compile a list of descriptive words about the whale and capture them on the whiteboard. (For instance, tired, anxious, determined.) How might he feel when he sees Michael? (Pleased, excited, relieved?) What is his aim or intention? (To pass on his message and avoid being stranded.)
- Ask the children to scan the text, noting any details that might be useful. For example, when the whale stares at Michael what might he be thinking? (Perhaps that Michael looks just right for his mission?)
- The children should then draft a paragraph describing the episode in the whale's words.

Differentiation
For older/more confident learners: Encourage the children to use their senses and include descriptive language.
For younger/less confident learners: Model a line in the whale's voice to help the children begin, such as: *I was swimming towards the great bridge when I saw a boy standing by the river.*

Get writing

SECTION 6

Whale facts

Objective: To summarise and shape material and ideas from different sources to write convincing and informative non-narrative texts.
What you need: Copies of *This Morning I Met a Whale*, whiteboard, individual whiteboards and pens.
Cross-curricular links: Science, geography.

What to do
- Ask the class to volunteer any facts about whales that we learn from the novel. List their ideas on the whiteboard and encourage them to examine whether the facts relate to appearance, habitat, behaviour, and so on.
- Explain to the children that they are going to use the novel to find out as many facts about whales as they can, in order to write a non-chronological report about whales. Before they begin, briefly revise the key features of report writing, such as present-tense verbs, generic participants, general statements to open and close.
- Arrange the children into pairs and allow them time to scan the story, writing down all the facts that they learn about whales on their individual whiteboards. Bring the class together to share their findings, listing them on the whiteboard.
- Challenge the children to work independently and use the facts to write an informative report on whales, including information on whale schools or family groups, how they communicate and breathe, and so on.

Differentiation
For older/more confident learners: Encourage the children to expand their research on whales using non-fiction books and the internet, and to use this information in their reports.
For younger/less confident learners: Provide page references to help the children locate key information on whales.

Rescue plan

Objective: To write non-narrative texts using structures of different text types.
What you need: Copies of *This Morning I Met a Whale*, whiteboard and photocopiable page 29.
Cross-curricular link: Science.

What to do
- Inform the children that they are going to focus on the rescue effort that is launched when the whale is sighted in the Thames. Ask questions such as: *How is the whale in danger?* (It has come into shallow water and is at risk of being stranded.) *What is the aim of the rescue attempt?* (To get it safely into deeper water so that it can swim back out to sea.)
- Arrange the class into pairs and provide them with photocopiable page 29. Explain that they need to scan the text from *By the time Michael arrived…* to the end of the novel, noting down key details about the rescue attempt, including the experts involved, the methods used and the different stages of the rescue attempt.
- After the children have completed the photocopiable sheet, bring the class together and review the key facts about the rescue effort.
- Finally, let the children work individually using their notes to draft a report on the rescue plan, explaining who was involved and the methods they used to try to return the whale to the sea.

Differentiation
For older/more confident learners: Challenge the children to use their notes to draft an instruction leaflet that could have been issued to the rescue team.
For younger/less confident learners: Limit the children to completing half the sheet, focusing on explaining the aim and the experts involved in the rescue. Then allow them to work in their pairs to draft the report.

Get writing

SECTION 6

Michael's diary

Objective: To make decisions about form and purpose, identify success criteria and then use them to evaluate their writing.
What you need: Copies of *This Morning I Met a Whale*, individual whiteboards and pens.
Cross-curricular link: PSHE.

What to do
- Remind the children that the events described in *This Morning I Met a Whale* span the course of one day, beginning at 5am and ending after dark. Invite them to create a diary entry that Michael might write, recording the day. The diary entry will cover the same events and time span as the book but must be much more concise.
- Briefly re-cap diary form and, as a shared activity, compile a checklist of criteria for assessing an effective diary entry. For example:
  - first person?
  - past tense?
  - records all main events?
  - concise?
  - informative/entertaining?
- Ask the children to summarise the main events that Michael would want to include, such as:
  - What happened when he saw the whale?
  - What happened in class?
  - What happened during the rescue effort?
- Allow the children time to draft their entries and then invite volunteers to read them to the class. Encourage assessment using the checklist.

Differentiation
For older/more confident learners: Ask the children to expand the diary entry by describing Michael's feelings during the day, as well as the main events.
For younger/less confident learners: As a shared activity with the children, compile a list of key events to include in the diary entry before they begin.

The whale's journey

Objective: To develop and refine ideas in writing using planning and problem-solving strategies.
What you need: Copies of *This Morning I Met a Whale*, photocopiable page 30 and a map of Northern Europe showing Iceland and the UK.
Cross-curricular link: Geography.

What to do
- Ask the children if they can recall where Michael thinks the whale has come from (the North Atlantic, near Iceland or Scotland).
- Display a map of Northern Europe and encourage the children to suggest a possible route for the whale, south-east from Iceland down to the Thames estuary. What distance do they think he might have swum? Can they suggest a way of roughly assessing this? (Find out the distance from Reykjavik to London – nearly 2000 kilometres or 1200 miles.)
- Arrange the children into pairs and hand out photocopiable page 30. Explain that they are going to label the map with details of what the whale might have seen on his journey south. They could include coastal towns or cities, or things like oil rigs, ships, barges and lighthouses.
- Next, encourage the children to work individually to write a paragraph in the whale's voice, describing his journey and the things he saw along the way.
- Invite volunteers to read their descriptions to the class and encourage constructive feedback.

Differentiation
For older/more confident learners: Encourage the children to explore maps and guides to help them add accurate details to their map.
For younger/less confident learners: Allow the children to concentrate on a few details of the journey, drawing sketches with labels (for example, an oil rig, fishing boat, ferry or lighthouse).

Get writing

SECTION 6

Bird-spotter's guide

- Research one type of waterbird and complete the details below for a bird-spotter's guide.

Name of bird: _____

Appearance and size: _____
_____
_____
_____
_____

Diet: _____
_____
_____
_____
_____

Habitat: _____
_____
_____
_____
_____

Notes on behaviour: _____
_____
_____
_____
_____

Any other details: _____
_____
_____
_____
_____

READ & RESPOND: Activities based on This Morning I Met a Whale

Get writing

SECTION 6

Rescue plan

- Gather details about the rescue attempt using the prompts below.

Briefly explain the aim of the rescue attempt.

_____

_____

List the experts or services involved and briefly explain their role in the rescue.

Expert/service	Role

Summarise the main stages in the rescue.

1. _____

_____

2. _____

_____

Explain the main risks to the whale.

_____

_____

Get writing

SECTION 6

The whale's journey

- Plot the whale's journey from Iceland to the Thames estuary. Label key places and things he might see on the way.

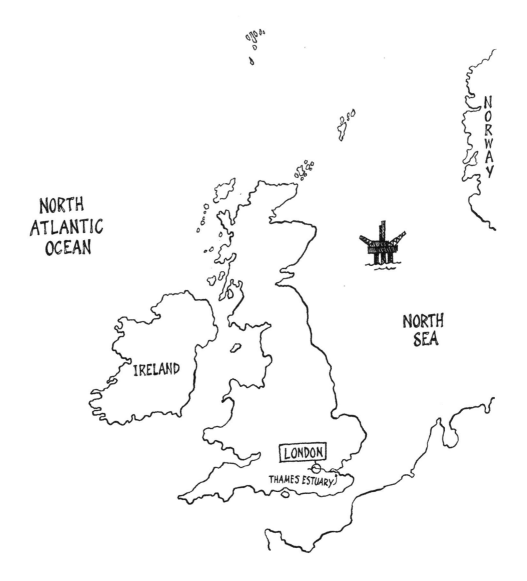

Assessment

SECTION 7

Assessment advice

This Morning I Met a Whale demonstrates how the author adapts and transforms real events into fiction, investing the whale with a purpose and personalising the story through Michael, a boy narrator, charged with passing on the whale's message to the world. Environmental issues are a recurrent theme in Morpurgo's work and this novel provides several opportunities for cross-curricular links with science and geography. It also allows children to explore narrative voice, as it shifts from first to third person, and has features of memoir or autobiographical writing, recounting a day in a life.

In the *Read & Respond* series, children carry out a range of activities to exercise their speaking, listening, reading and writing skills. Assessment should be an on-going process, recording progress and highlighting areas that need improvement. It should be based on contributions in shared class work as well as on written individual, paired or group work. At the end of each lesson, encourage the children to assess their own work against the objectives set, and to decide which areas need further practice. They should also be encouraged to provide constructive feedback for writing partners and groups.

The children can create their own assessment activities, such as compiling spelling tests based on parts of speech (nouns, adjectives or verbs), technical terms or topics such as river scenery or whales. They could work in pairs or groups to compile true or false statements about the book, then challenge their partner or another group to decide on answers. Photocopiable page 32 is a book review, and can be used as an assessment activity.

Book review

Assessment focus: To read extensively favourite authors/genres and experiment with other types of text.
What you need: Whiteboard and photocopiable page 32.

What to do
● Ask the children if they enjoyed reading *This Morning I Met a Whale* and, if so, why.
● Discuss their favourite parts of the story. Which parts did they find most tense or exciting? Which parts were sad? Which were thought-provoking?
● Do the children understand what the main themes of the story are? (Friendship or the bond between boy and whale, environmental issues, the interdependent relationship between people and nature?) Write their suggestions on the whiteboard.
● If there is time, these themes can be explored in other novels by the same author and parallels identified. (For example, *The Butterfly Lion* and *Born to Run* explore the bonds between humans and wild animals, while the rescue of wild animals features in *Why the Whales Came*, *The Wreck of the Zanzibar* and *Kensuke's Kingdom*.)
● Encourage the children to explore other genres with environmental themes, including non-fiction, considering which have the most impact in provoking thought and inspiring change.
● Challenge the children to work independently to complete the book review on photocopiable page 32.
● When they have finished, use them to initiate a class review of the novel, encouraging the children to compare and contrast it with other novels they have read by Michael Morpurgo.

Assessment

Book review

- Complete the book review below for *This Morning I Met a Whale*.

Write some blurb that summarises the story and persuades others to read the novel.

_____

_____

_____

Write examples of events that are:

Surprising: _____

_____

Tense: _____

_____

Sad: _____

_____

What is your favourite part of the story and why?

_____

_____

_____

How do these themes feature in the plot?

Friendship: _____

Bravery: _____

Solemn promises: _____

Give the book a star rating out of 5: ☆ ☆ ☆ ☆ ☆